The Intellectuals and Socialism

The IEA Health and Welfare Unit

Rediscovered Riches No. 4

The Intellectuals and Socialism

Friedrich A. Hayek

Foreword by
Edwin J. Feulner Jr.

Introduction by
John Blundell

IEA Health and Welfare Unit
London

Published October 1998

The IEA Health and Welfare Unit
2 Lord North St
London SW1P 3LB

Typeset by the IEA Health and Welfare Unit
in Bookman 10 point
Printed in Great Britain by
St Edmundsbury Press
Bury St Edmunds, Suffolk

Contents

Page

The Authors   vi

Foreword
  Edwin J. Feulner Jr.   vii

Introduction
  John Blundell   1

The Intellectuals and Socialism
  F.A. Hayek   7

The Authors

Friedrich A. Hayek (1899-1992) was born in Vienna and obtained two doctorates from the University of Vienna, in law and political economy. He worked under Ludwig von Mises at the Austrian Institute for Business Cycle Research, and from 1929-31 was a lecturer in economics at the University of Vienna. His first book, *Monetary Theory and the Trade Cycle*, was published in 1929. In 1931 Hayek was made Tooke Professor of Economic Science and Statistics at the London School of Economics, and in 1950 he was appointed Professor of Social and Moral Sciences at the University of Chicago. In 1962 he was appointed Professor of Political Economy at the University of Freiburg where he became Professor Emeritus in 1967. Hayek was elected a Fellow of the British Academy in 1944, and in 1947 he organised the conference in Switzerland which resulted in the creation of the Mont Pèlerin Society. He was awarded the Nobel Prize in Economics in 1974 and was created a Companion of Honour in 1984. In 1991 George Bush presented Hayek with the Presidential Medal of Freedom. His books include *The Pure Theory of Capital*, 1941, *The Road to Serfdom*, 1944, *The Counter-Revolution of Science*, 1952, *The Constitution of Liberty*, 1960, *Law, Legislation and Liberty*, 1973-9, and *The Fatal Conceit*, 1988.

John Blundell is General Director of the Institute of Economic Affairs. He was previously President of the Institute for Humane Studies at George Mason University and the Atlas Economic Research Foundation, founded by the late Sir Antony Fisher to establish 'sister' organisations to the IEA. He serves on the Boards of both organisations as well as on the board of the Mont Pèlerin Society.

Edwin J. Feulner has served as President of The Heritage Foundation since 1977. He is also the immediate past President of the Mont Pèlerin Society. He previously served in high level positions in both the legislative and executive branch of the federal government. He received his Ph.D. from the University of Edinburgh and was awarded the Presidential Citizen's Medal by Ronald Reagan in 1989 for 'being a leader of the conservative movement by building an organisation dedicated to ideas and their consequences...'

Foreword

Edwin J. Feulner Jr.

IN THE LATE Professor F.A. Hayek's 1949 essay, 'The Intellectuals and Socialism', the author's final paragraph warns: 'Unless we can make the philosophic foundations of a free society once more a living intellectual issue, and its implementation a task which challenges the ingenuity and imagination of our liveliest minds, the prospects of freedom are indeed dark. But if we can regain that belief in the power of ideas which was the mark of liberalism at its best, the battle is not lost. The intellectual revival of liberalism is already under way in many parts of the world. Will it be in time?'

Fortunately, Professor Hayek's warning was heeded, *just* in time. His colleagues in the Mont Pèlerin Society, his students, and his admirers from around the world took his message to heart, and they have spent the decades since the publication of this essay honing their arguments for liberty, and transmitting these ideas through institutions, publications and conferences with a success undreamt of in 1949.

For many of us, Hayek's brief essay was a call to action. In it, he explained the process by which ideas are developed and become widely accepted, and he noted why our own classical liberal ideas may not be as widely held, or as fashionable, as they deserve to be. For too long we had underestimated the power of the 'intellectual class'—the 'professional second-hand dealers in ideas', as Hayek refers to them—to shape the climate of public opinion. As Hayek pointed out, the parties of the Left directed most of their energies, either by design or circumstance, toward gaining the support of this intellectual élite—the journalists, teachers, ministers, lecturers, publicists, writers, and artists who were masters of the technique of conveying ideas. At the time of this essay Hayek said that most of us learn little about events or ideas except through this class (and with the growth of television, it's probably even less). The intellectuals have become gatekeepers for the information, views, and opinions that ultimately do reach us. Conservatives, by contrast, had concentrated on reaching and persuading individual voters.

For many of us, this essay was a challenge to build up our own class of intellectuals made up of those who loved liberty. We trained, hired, networked, and supported academics, policy analysts, journalists, radio talk show hosts, and even political leaders who would shape public opinion and influence the politics of tomorrow. And in many areas we have succeeded in changing the climate of public opinion *and* changing the world. Communism has failed, the Berlin Wall has been torn down, and even left-of-centre politicians like President Clinton and Prime Minister Blair are embracing the rhetoric of our classical liberal solutions when talking of some of our modern social problems. I believe the irony would not be lost on Professor Hayek!

Clearly much remains to be done before we can enjoy a truly free society. And for guidance we should once again turn to Hayek. As he points out, much of the success socialism gained up until 1949 was not by engaging in a battle of conflicting ideals, but by contrasting the existing state of affairs with that one ideal of a possible future society which the socialists alone held up before the public. 'Very few of the other programmes which offered themselves provided genuine alternatives.' (p. 22.) Compromises were thus made somewhere between the socialist ideal and the existing state of affairs. The only questions for socialists were how fast and how far to proceed. Conservatives have learned this lesson: it is not enough to stop bad policies, we have to offer genuine alternatives.

Since the original publication of 'The Intellectuals and Social-ism' we have developed the philosophical foundations of a free society, thanks to Hayek, our friends at the IEA, and others. And we have built a class of intellectuals to translate these philosoph-ical ideas to the public. However, we have not held up before the public our own vision of a future society built on liberty. And this is the task facing us as we approach the new millennium. As Hayek said, the task of constructing a free society can be exciting and fascinating. If we are to succeed, we must make the building of a free society once more an intellectual adventure and a deed of courage.

As an *alumnus* of the Institute of Economic Affairs, I particu-larly thank our good friends at the IEA for re-publishing this very special essay, and most importantly for the many courageous intellectual adventures they have undertaken in their 40 years.

Introduction

Hayek and the Second-hand Dealers in Ideas

John Blundell

IN APRIL 1945 *Reader's Digest* published the condensed version of Friedrich Hayek's classic work *The Road to Serfdom*. For the first and still the only time in the history of the *Digest*, the condensed book was carried at the front of the magazine rather than the back.

Among the many who read the condensed book was Antony Fisher. In his very early thirties, this former Battle of Britain pilot turned stockbroker turned farmer went to see Hayek at the London School of Economics to discuss his concern over the advance of socialism and collectivism in Britain. Fisher feared that the country for whom so many, including his father and brother, had died in two world wars in order that it should remain free was, in fact, becoming less and less free. He saw liberty threatened by the ever-growing power and scope of the state. The purpose of his visit to Hayek, the great architect of the revival of classical liberal ideas, was to ask what could be done about it.

My central question was what, if anything, could he advise me to do to help get discussion and policy on the right lines... Hayek first warned me against wasting time—as I was then tempted—by taking up a political career. He explained his view that the decisive influence in the battle of ideas and policy was wielded by intellectuals whom he characterised as the 'second-hand dealers in ideas'. It was the dominant intellectuals from the Fabians onwards who had tilted the political debate in favour of growing government intervention with all that followed. If I shared the view that better ideas were not getting a fair hearing, his counsel was that I should join with others in forming a scholarly research organisation to supply intellectuals in

1

universities, schools, journalism and broadcasting with authoritative studies of the economic theory of markets and its application to practical affairs.[1]

Fisher went on to make his fortune by introducing factory farming of chickens on the American model to Britain. His company, Buxted Chickens, changed the diet of his fellow countrymen, and made him rich enough to carry out Hayek's advice. He set up the Institute of Economic Affairs in 1955 with the view that:

> [T]hose carrying on intellectual work must have a considerable impact through newspapers, radio, television and so on, on the thinking of the average individual. *Socialism was spread in this way and it is time we started to reverse the process.*[2]

He thus set himself exactly the task which Hayek had recommended to him in 1945.

****

Soon after that meeting with Fisher, Hayek expanded on his theory of the influence of intellectuals in an essay entitled 'The Intellectuals and Socialism', first published in the *Chicago Law Review* in 1949 and now republished by the Institute of Economic Affairs. According to Hayek, the intellectual is neither an original thinker nor an expert. Indeed he need not even be intelligent. What he does possess is:

a)   the ability to speak/write on a wide range of subjects; and
b)   a way of becoming familiar with new ideas earlier than his audience.

Let me attempt to summarise Hayek's insights:

1.   Pro-market ideas had failed to remain relevant and inspiring, thus opening the door to anti-market forces.

2.   Peoples' knowledge of history plays a much greater role in the development of their political philosophy than we normally think.[3]

3.   Practical men and women concerned with the minutiae of today's events tend to lose sight of long-term considerations.

4.   Be alert to special interests, especially those that, while claiming to be pro-free enterprise in general, always want to make exceptions in their own areas of expertise.

5. The outcome of today's politics is already set, so look for leverage for tomorrow as a scholar or intellectual.

6. The intellectual is the gatekeeper of ideas.

7. The best pro-market people become businessmen, engineers, doctors and so on; the best anti-market people become intellectuals and scholars.

8. Be Utopian and believe in the power of ideas.

Hayek's primary example is the period 1850 to 1950 during which socialism was nowhere, at first, a working-class movement. There was always a long-term effort by the intellectuals before the working classes accepted socialism. Indeed all countries that have turned to socialism experienced an earlier phase in which for many years socialist ideas governed the thinking of more active intellectuals. Once you reach this phase, experience suggests, it is just a matter of time before the views of today's intellectuals become tomorrow's politics.

'The Intellectuals and Socialism' was published in 1949 but, apart from one reference in one sentence, there is nothing to say it could not have been written 40 years later, just before Hayek's death. It might have been written 40 years earlier but for the fact that, as a young man, he felt the over-generous instincts of socialism. When Hayek penned his thoughts, socialism seemed triumphant across the world. Anybody of enlightened sensibility regarded themselves as of 'The Left'. To be of 'The Right' was to be morally deformed, foolish, or both.

In Alan Bennett's 1968 play *Forty Years On* the Headmaster of Albion House, a minor public school which represents Britain, asks: 'Why is it always the intelligent people who are socialists?'[4] Hayek's answer, which he expressed in his last major work, *The Fatal Conceit*, was that 'intelligent people will tend to overvalue intelligence'. They think that everything worth knowing can be discovered by processes of intellectual examination and 'find it hard to believe that there can exist any useful knowledge that did not originate in deliberate experimentation'. They consequently neglect the 'traditional rules', the 'second endowment' of 'cultural evolution' which, for Hayek, included morals, especially 'our institutions of property, freedom and justice'. They think that any imperfection can be corrected by 'rational coordination' and this leads them 'to be favourably disposed to the central economic planning and control that lie at the heart of socialism'. Thus, whether or not they call themselves socialists, 'the higher we climb up the ladder of intelligence ... the more likely we are to encounter socialist convictions'.[5]

****

Only when you start to list all the different groups of intellectuals do you realise how many there are, how their role has grown in modern times, and how dependent we have become on them. The more obvious ones are those who are professionals at conveying a message but are amateurs when it comes to substance. They include the 'journalists, teachers, ministers, lecturers, publicists, radio commentators, writers of fiction, cartoonists, and artists'. However we should also note the role of 'professional men and technicians' (p. 11) who are listened to by others with respect on topics outside their competence because of their standing. The intellectuals decide what we hear, in what form we are to hear it and from what angle it is to be presented. They decide who will be heard and who will not be heard. The supremacy and pervasiveness of television as the controlling medium of modern culture makes that even more true of our own day than it was in the 1940s.

There is an alarming sentence in this essay: '[I]n most parts of the Western World even the most determined opponents of socialism derive from socialist sources their knowledge on most subjects on which they have no first-hand information' (p. 14). Division of knowledge is a part of the division of labour. Knowledge, and its manipulation, are the bulk of much labour now. A majority earns its living in services of myriad sorts rather than in manufacturing or agriculture.

A liberal, or as Hayek would always say, a Whig, cannot disagree with a socialist analysis in a field in which he has no knowledge. The disquieting theme of Hayek's argument is how the fragmentation of knowledge is a tactical boon to socialists. Experts in particular fields often gain 'rents' from state intervention and, while overtly free-market in their outlook elsewhere, are always quick to explain why the market does not work in their area.

This was one of the reasons for establishing the IEA and its 100-plus sister bodies around the world. Hayek also regarded the creation of the Mont Pèlerin Society, which first met in 1947, as an opportunity for minds engaged in the fight against socialism to exchange ideas—meaning, by socialism, all those ideas devoted to empowering the state. The threat posed by the forces of coercion to those of voluntary association or spontaneous action is what concerned him.

The struggle has become more difficult as policy makers have become less and less willing to identify themselves explicitly as socialists. A review of a book on socialism which appeared in 1885 began:

> Socialism is the hobby of the day. Platform and study resound with the word, and street and debating society inscribe it on their banners.[6]

How unlike the home life of our own New Labour! Socialism has become the 's' word, and was not mentioned in the Labour Party's election manifesto.[7]

Socialism survives, however, by transmuting itself into new forms. State-run enterprises are now frowned upon, but the ever-expanding volume of regulation—financial, environmental, health and safety—serves to empower the state by other means.

****

Part of Hayek's charm is the pull of his sheer geniality. He is generous and mannerly in acknowledging that most socialists have benign intentions. They are blind to the real flaws of their recipes. Typically, Hayek ends with a point in their favour: '[I]t was their courage to be Utopian which gained them the support of the intellectuals and therefore an influence on public opinion' (p. 26). Those who concern themselves exclusively with what seems practicable are marginalised by the greater influence of prevailing opinion.

I commend to you Hayek's urge not to seek compromises. We can leave that to the politicians. 'Free trade and freedom of opportunity are ideals which still may arouse the imaginations of large numbers, but a mere "reasonable freedom of trade" or a mere "relaxation of controls" is neither intellectually respectable nor likely to inspire any enthusiasm' (p. 26).

Most of the readers of this paper will be Hayek's 'second-hand dealers in ideas'. Conceit makes us all prone to believe we are original thinkers but Hayek explains that we are mostly transmitters of ideas borrowed from earlier minds (hence second-hand, in a non-pejorative sense). Those scholars who really are the founts of new ideas are far more rare than we all suppose. However,

Hayek argues that we, and the world, are governed by ideas and that we can only expand our political and policy horizons by deploying them.

He was supported in this view—and it was probably the only view they shared—by John Maynard Keynes. In 1936 Keynes had concluded his most famous book, *The General Theory of Employment, Interest and Money*, with these ringing words:

> ... the ideas of economists and political philosophers, both when they are right and when they are wrong, are more powerful than is commonly understood. Indeed the world is ruled by little else. Practical men, who believe themselves to be quite exempt from any intellectual influences, are usually the slaves of some defunct economist ... Soon or late, it is ideas, not vested interests, which are dangerous for good or evil.[8]

Of course, this was true of no one more than of Keynes himself, whose followers were wreaking havoc with the world's economies long after he had become defunct. But it was also true of Hayek. It was Hayek's great good fortune to live long enough to see his own ideas enter the mainstream of public policy debate. They were not always attributed to him: they were described as Thatcherism, or Adam-Smith liberalism, or neo-conservatism, but he was responsible for their re-emergence, whether credited or not. We received a striking demonstration of this at the IEA in 1996 when we invited Donald Brash, the Governor of the Reserve Bank of New Zealand, to give the prestigious Annual Hayek Memorial Lecture on the subject of 'New Zealand's Remarkable Reforms'. He admitted that, although 'the New Zealand reforms have a distinctly Hayekian flavour', the architects of them were scarcely aware of Hayek at all, and Brash himself had never read a word of Hayek before being asked to give the lecture.[9]

The IEA can claim some victories in the increasing awareness of classical liberal ideas and ideals. It is hard to measure our influence, yet, if we awaken some young scholar to the possibility that the paradigms or conventions of a discipline may be flawed, we can change the life of that mind forever. If we convince a young journalist he can do more good, and have more fun, by criticising the remnants of our socialist inheritance, we can change that life. If we persuade a young politician he can harass the forces of inertia by tackling privilege and bureaucracy, we change the course of that life too. The IEA continues in its mission to move around the furniture in the minds of intellectuals. That includes you, probably.

The Intellectuals and Socialism

F.A. Hayek

A Note on the Text

'The Intellectuals and Socialism' was first published in the *University of Chicago Law Review*, Vol. 16, No. 3, Spring 1949. It was reprinted in *Studies in Philosophy, Politics and Economics*, F.A. Hayek, London: Routledge and Kegan Paul, 1967. It was published as a booklet in the Studies in Social Theory Series by the Institute of Humane Studies, California, 1971. The text of this edition is taken from *Studies in Philosophy, Politics and Economics*. The copyright of 'The Intellectuals and Socialism' remains with the University of Chicago, and the essay is republished here by kind permission.

I

IN ALL DEMOCRATIC countries, in the United States even more than elsewhere, a strong belief prevails that the influence of the intellectuals on politics is negligible. This is no doubt true of the power of intellectuals to make their peculiar opinions of the moment influence decisions, of the extent to which they can sway the popular vote on questions on which they differ from the current views of the masses. Yet over somewhat longer periods they have probably never exercised so great an influence as they do today in those countries. This power they wield by shaping public opinion.

In the light of recent history it is somewhat curious that this decisive power of the professional second-hand dealers in ideas should not yet be more generally recognised. The political development of the Western world during the last hundred years furnishes the clearest demonstration. Socialism has never and nowhere been at first a working-class movement. It is by no means an obvious remedy for the obvious evil which the interests of that class will necessarily demand. It is a construction of theorists, deriving from certain tendencies of abstract thought with which for a long time only the intellectuals were familiar; and it required long efforts by the intellectuals before the working classes could be persuaded to adopt it as their programme.

In every country that has moved toward socialism, the phase of the development in which socialism becomes a determining influence on politics has been preceded for many years by a period during which socialist ideals governed the thinking of the more active intellectuals. In Germany this stage had been reached towards the end of the last century; in England and France, about the time of the First World War. To the casual observer it would seem as if the United States had reached this phase after World War II and that the attraction of a planned and directed economic system is now as strong among the American intellectuals as it ever was among their German or English fellows. Experience suggests that, once this phase has been reached, it is merely a question of time until the views now held by the intellectuals become the governing force of politics.

The character of the process by which the views of the intellectuals influence the politics of tomorrow is therefore of much more than academic interest. Whether we merely wish to foresee or attempt to influence the course of events, it is a factor of much greater importance than is generally understood. What to the contemporary observer appears as the battle of conflicting interests has indeed often been decided long before in a clash of ideas confined to narrow circles. Paradoxically enough, however, in general the parties of the Left have done most to spread the belief that it was the numerical strength of the opposing material interests which decided political issues, whereas in practice these same parties have regularly and successfully acted as if they understood the key position of the intellectuals. Whether by design or driven by the force of circumstances, they have always directed their main effort towards gaining the support of this 'élite', while the more conservative groups have acted, as regularly but unsuccessfully, on a more naïve view of mass democracy and have usually vainly tried directly to reach and to persuade the individual voter.

II

The term 'intellectuals', however, does not at once convey a true picture of the large class to which we refer, and the fact that we have no better name by which to describe what we have called the second-hand dealers in ideas is not the least of the reasons why their power is not better understood. Even persons who use the word 'intellectual' mainly as a term of abuse are still inclined to withhold it from many who undoubtedly perform that characteristic function. This is neither that of the original thinker nor that of the scholar or expert in a particular field of thought. The typical intellectual need be neither: he need not possess special knowledge of anything in particular, nor need he even be particularly intelligent, to perform his role as intermediary in the spreading of ideas. What qualifies him for his job is the wide range of subjects on which he can readily talk and write, and a position or habits through which he becomes acquainted with new ideas sooner than those to whom he addresses himself.

Until one begins to list all the professions and activities which belong to this class, it is difficult to realise how numerous it is, how the scope for its activities constantly increases in modern society, and how dependent on it we all have become. The class does not consist only of journalists, teachers, ministers, lecturers, publicists, radio commentators, writers of fiction, cartoonists, and artists—all of whom may be masters of the technique of conveying ideas but are usually amateurs so far as the substance of what they convey is concerned. The class also includes many professional men and technicians, such as scientists and doctors, who through their habitual intercourse with the printed word become carriers of new ideas outside their own fields and who, because of their expert knowledge of their own subjects, are listened to with respect on most others. There is little that the ordinary man of today learns about events or ideas except through the medium of this class; and outside our special fields of work we are in this respect almost all ordinary men, dependent for our information and instruction on those who make it their job to keep abreast of opinion. It is the intellectuals in this sense who decide what views and opinions are to reach us, which facts are important enough to be told to us, and in what form and from what angle they are to be presented. Whether we shall ever learn of the results of the work of the expert and the original thinker depends mainly on their decision.

The layman, perhaps, is not fully aware to what extent even the popular reputations of scientists and scholars are made by that class and are inevitably affected by its views on subjects which have little to do with the merits of the real achievements. And it is specially significant for our problem that every scholar can probably name several instances from his field of men who have undeservedly achieved a popular reputation as great scientists solely because they hold what the intellectuals regard as 'progressive' political views; but I have yet to come across a single instance where such a scientific pseudo-reputation has been bestowed for political reason on a scholar of more conservative leanings. This creation of reputations by the intellectuals is particularly important in the fields where the results of expert studies are not used by other specialists but depend on the political decision of the public at large. There is indeed scarcely a better illustration of this than the attitude which professional economists have taken to the growth of such doctrines as socialism or protectionism. There was probably at no time a majority of economists, who were recognised as such by their peers, favourable to socialism (or, for that matter, to protection).

In all probability it is even true to say that no other similar group of students contains so high a proportion of its members decidedly opposed to socialism (or protection). This is the more significant as in recent times it is as likely as not that it was an early interest in socialist schemes for reform which led a man to choose economics for his profession. Yet it is not the predominant views of the experts but the views of a minority, mostly of rather doubtful standing in their profession, which are taken up and spread by the intellectuals.

The all-pervasive influence of the intellectuals in contemporary society is still further strengthened by the growing importance of 'organisation'. It is a common but probably mistaken belief that the increase of organisation increases the influence of the expert or specialist. This may be true of the expert administrator and organiser, if there are such people, but hardly of the expert in any particular field of knowledge. It is rather the person whose general knowledge is supposed to qualify him to appreciate expert testimony, and to judge between the experts from different fields, whose power is enhanced. The point which is important for us, however, is that the scholar who becomes a university president, the scientist who takes charge of an institute or foundation, the scholar who becomes an editor or the active promoter of an organisation serving a particular cause, all rapidly cease to be scholars or experts and become intellectuals in our sense, people who judge all issues not by their specific merits but, in the characteristic manner of intellectuals, solely in the light of certain fashionable general ideas. The number of such institutions which breed intellectuals and increase their number and powers grows every day. Almost all the 'experts' in the mere technique of getting knowledge over are, with respect to the subject matter which they handle, intellectuals and not experts.

In the sense in which we are using the term, the intellectuals are in fact a fairly new phenomenon of history. Though nobody will regret that education has ceased to be a privilege of the propertied classes, the fact that the propertied classes are no longer the best educated and the fact that the large number of people who owe their position solely to their general education do not possess that experience of the working of the economic system which the administration of property gives, are important for understanding the role of the intellectual. Professor Schumpeter, who has devoted an illuminating chapter of his *Capitalism,*

Socialism, and Democracy to some aspects of our problem, has not unfairly stressed that it is the absence of direct responsibility for practical affairs and the consequent absence of first-hand knowledge of them which distinguishes the typical intellectual from other people who also wield the power of the spoken and written word. It would lead too far, however, to examine here further the development of this class and the curious claim which has recently been advanced by one of its theorists that it was the only one whose views were not decidedly influenced by its own economic interests. One of the important points that would have to be examined in such a discussion would be how far the growth of this class has been artificially stimulated by the law of copyright.[1]

III

It is not surprising that the real scholar or expert and the practical man of affairs often feel contemptuous about the intellectual, are disinclined to recognise his power, and are resentful when they discover it. Individually they find the intellectuals mostly to be people who understand nothing in particular especially well and whose judgement on matters they themselves understand shows little sign of special wisdom. But it would be a fatal mistake to underestimate their power for this reason. Even though their knowledge may be often superficial and their intelligence limited, this does not alter the fact that it is their judgement which mainly determines the views on which society will act in the not too distant future. It is no exaggeration to say that, once the more active part of the intellectuals has been converted to a set of beliefs, the process by which these become generally accepted is almost automatic and irresistible. These intellectuals are the organs which modern society has developed for spreading knowledge and ideas, and it is their convictions and opinions which operate as the sieve through which all new conceptions must pass before they can reach the masses.

It is of the nature of the intellectual's job that he must use his own knowledge and convictions in performing his daily task. He occupies his position because he possesses, or has had to deal from day to day with, knowledge which his employer in general does not possess, and his activities can therefore be directed by others only to a limited extent. And just because the intellectuals are mostly intellectually honest, it is inevitable that they should follow their own convictions whenever they have discretion and that they should give a corresponding slant to everything that passes through their hands. Even where the direction of policy is in the hands of men of affairs of different views, the execution of policy will in general be in the hands of intellectuals, and it is frequently the decision on the detail which determines the net effect. We find this illustrated in almost all fields of contemporary society. Newspapers in 'capitalist' ownership, universities presided over by 'reactionary' governing bodies, broadcasting systems owned by conservative governments, have all been known to influence public opinion in the direction of socialism, because this was the conviction of the personnel. This has often happened not only in spite of, but perhaps even because of, the attempts of those at the top to control opinion and to impose principles of orthodoxy.

The effect of this filtering of ideas through the convictions of a class which is constitutionally disposed to certain views is by no means confined to the masses. Outside his special field the expert is generally no less dependent on this class and scarcely less influenced by their selection. The result of this is that today in most parts of the Western world even the most determined opponents of socialism derive from socialist sources their knowledge on most subjects on which they have no first-hand information. With many of the more general preconceptions of socialist thought, the connection of their more practical proposals is by no means at once obvious; in consequence, many men who believe themselves to be determined opponents of that system of thought become in fact effective spreaders of its ideas. Who does not know the practical man who in his own field denounces socialism as 'pernicious rot' but, when he steps outside his subject, spouts socialism like any Left journalist?

In no other field has the predominant influence of the socialist intellectuals been felt more strongly during the last hundred years than in the contacts between different national civilisations. It would go far beyond the limits of this article to trace the causes and significance of the highly important fact that in the modern world the intellectuals provide almost the only approach to an international community. It is this which mainly accounts for the extraordinary spectacle that for generations the supposedly 'capitalist' West has been lending its moral and material support almost exclusively to those ideological movements in the countries farther east which aimed at undermining Western civilisation and that, at the same time, the information which the Western public has obtained about events in Central and Eastern Europe has almost inevitably been coloured by a socialist bias. Many of the 'educational' activities of the American forces of occupation in Germany have furnished clear and recent examples of this tendency.

IV

A proper understanding of the reasons which tend to incline so many of the intellectuals towards socialism is thus most important. The first point here which those who do not share this bias ought to face frankly is that it is neither selfish interests nor evil intentions but mostly honest convictions and good intentions which determine the intellectuals' views. In fact, it is necessary to recognise that on the whole the typical intellectual is today more likely to be a socialist the more he is guided by good will and intelligence, and that on the plane of purely intellectual argument he will generally be able to make out a better case than the majority of his opponents within his class. If we still think him wrong, we must recognise that it may be genuine error which leads the well-meaning and intelligent people who occupy those key positions in our society to spread views which to us appear a threat to our civilisation.[2] Nothing could be more important than to try to understand the sources of this error in order that we should be able to counter it. Yet those who are generally regarded as the representatives of the existing order and who believe that they comprehend the dangers of socialism are usually very far from such understanding. They tend to regard the socialist intellectuals as nothing more than a pernicious bunch of highbrow radicals without appreciating their influence and, by their whole attitude to them, tend to drive them even further into opposition to the existing order.

If we are to understand this peculiar bias of a large section of the intellectuals, we must be clear about two points. The first is that they generally judge all particular issues exclusively in the light of certain general ideas; the second, that the characteristic errors of any age are frequently derived from some genuine new truths it has discovered, and they are erroneous applications of new generalisations which have proved their value in other fields.

The conclusion to which we shall be led by a full consideration of these facts will be that the effective refutation of such errors will frequently require further intellectual advance, and often advance on points which are very abstract and may seem very remote from the practical issues.

It is perhaps the most characteristic feature of the intellectual that he judges new ideas not by their specific merits but by the readiness with which they fit into his general conceptions, into the picture of the world which he regards as modern or advanced. It is through their influence on him and on his choice of opinions on particular issues that the power of ideas for good and evil grows in proportion to their generality, abstractness, and even vagueness. As he knows little about the particular issues, his criterion must be consistency with his other views and suitability for combining into a coherent picture of the world. Yet this selection from the multitude of new ideas presenting themselves at every moment creates the characteristic climate of opinion, the dominant *Weltanschauung* of a period, which will be favourable to the reception of some opinions and unfavourable to others and which will make the intellectual readily accept one conclusion and reject another without a real understanding of the issues.

In some respects the intellectual is indeed closer to the philosopher than to any specialist, and the philosopher is in more than one sense a sort of prince among the intellectuals. Although his influence is farther removed from practical affairs and correspondingly slower and more difficult to trace than that of the ordinary intellectual, it is of the same kind and in the long run even more powerful than that of the latter. It is the same endeavour towards a synthesis, pursued more methodically, the same judgement of particular views in so far as they fit into a general system of thought rather than by their specific merits, the same striving after a consistent world view, which for both forms the main basis for accepting or rejecting ideas. For this reason the philosopher has probably a greater influence over the intellectuals than any other scholar or scientist and, more than anyone else, determines the manner in which the intellectuals exercise their censorship function. The popular influence of the scientific specialist begins to rival that of the philosopher only when he ceases to be a specialist and commences to philosophise about the progress of his subject—and usually only after he has been taken up by the intellectuals for reasons which have little to do with his scientific eminence.

The 'climate of opinion' of any period is thus essentially a set of very general preconceptions by which the intellectual judges the importance of new facts and opinions. These preconceptions are mainly applications to what seem to him the most significant aspects of scientific achievements, a transfer to other fields of what has particularly impressed him in the work of the special-ists. One could give a long list of such intellectual fashions and catchwords which in the course of two or three generations have in turn dominated the thinking of the intellectuals. Whether it was the 'historical approach' or the theory of evolution, nine-teenth century determinism and the belief in the predominant influence of environment as against heredity, the theory of relativity or the belief in the power of the unconscious—every one of these general conceptions has been made the touchstone by which innovations in different fields have been tested. It seems as if the less specific or precise (or the less understood) these ideas are, the wider may be their influence. Sometimes it is no more than a vague impression rarely put into words which thus wields a profound influence. Such beliefs as that deliberate control or conscious organisation is also in social affairs always superior to the results of spontaneous processes which are not directed by a human mind, or that any order based on a plan laid down beforehand must be better than one formed by the balancing of opposing forces, have in this way profoundly affected political development.

Only apparently different is the role of the intellectuals where the development of more properly social ideas is concerned. Here their peculiar propensities manifest themselves in making shibboleths of abstractions, in rationalising and carrying to extremes certain ambitions which spring from the normal intercourse of men. Since democracy is a good thing, the further the democratic principle can be carried, the better it appears to them. The most powerful of these general ideas which have shaped political development in recent times is of course the ideal of material equality. It is, characteristically, not one of the spontaneously grown moral convictions, first applied in the relations between particular individuals, but an intellectual construction originally conceived in the abstract and of doubtful meaning or application in particular instances. Nevertheless, it has operated strongly as a principle of selection among the alternative courses of social policy, exercising a persistent pressure towards an arrangement of social affairs which nobody clearly conceives. That a particular measure tends to bring about greater equality has come to be regarded as so strong a recommendation that little else will be considered. Since on each particular issue it is this one aspect on which those who guide opinion have a definite conviction, equality has determined social change even more strongly than its advocates intended.

Not only moral ideals act in this manner, however. Sometimes the attitudes of the intellectuals towards the problems of social order may be the consequence of advances in purely scientific knowledge, and it is in these instances that their erroneous views on particular issues may for a time seem to have all the prestige of the latest scientific achievements behind them. It is not in itself surprising that a genuine advance of knowledge should in this manner become on occasion a source of new error. If no false conclusions followed from new generalisations, they would be final truths which would never need revision. Although as a rule such a new generalisation will merely share the false consequences which can be drawn from it with the views which were held before, and thus not lead to new error, it is quite likely that a new theory, just as its value is shown by the valid new conclusions to which it leads, will produce other new conclusions which further advance will show to have been erroneous. But in such an instance a false belief will appear with all the prestige of the latest scientific knowledge supporting it. Although in the particular field to which this belief applies all the scientific evidence may be against it, it will nevertheless, before the tribunal of the intellectuals and in the light of the ideas which govern their thinking, be selected as the view which is best in accord with the spirit of the time. The specialists who will thus achieve public fame and wide influence will thus not be those who have gained recognition by their peers but will often be men whom the other experts regard as cranks, amateurs, or even frauds, but who in the eyes of the general public nevertheless become the best known exponents of their subject.

In particular, there can be little doubt that the manner in which during the last hundred years man has learned to organise the forces of nature has contributed a great deal towards the creation of the belief that a similar control of the forces of society would bring comparable improvements in human conditions. That, with the application of engineering techniques, the direction of all forms of human activity according to a single coherent plan should prove to be as successful in society as it has been in innumerable engineering tasks, is too plausible a conclusion not to seduce most of those who are elated by the achievement of the natural sciences. It must indeed be admitted both that it would require powerful arguments to counter the strong presumption in favour of such a conclusion and that these arguments have not yet been adequately stated. It is not sufficient to point out the defects of particular proposals based on this kind of reasoning. The argument will not lose its force until it has been conclusively shown why what has proved so eminently successful in producing advances in so many fields should have limits to its usefulness and become positively harmful if extended beyond these limits. This is a task which has not yet been satisfactorily performed and which will have to be achieved before this particular impulse towards socialism can be removed.

This, of course, is only one of many instances where further intellectual advance is needed if the harmful ideas at present current are to be refuted and where the course which we shall travel will ultimately be decided by the discussion of very abstract issues. It is not enough for the man of affairs to be sure, from his intimate knowledge of a particular field, that the theories of socialism which are derived from more general ideas will prove impracticable. He may be perfectly right, and yet his resistance will be overwhelmed and all the sorry consequences which he foresees will follow if he is not supported by an effective refutation of the *idées mères*. So long as the intellectual gets the better of the general argument, the most valid objections to the specific issue will be brushed aside.

V

This is not the whole story, however. The forces which influence recruitment to the ranks of the intellectuals operate in the same direction and help to explain why so many of the most able among them lean towards socialism. There are of course as many differences of opinion among intellectuals as among other groups of people; but it seems to be true that it is on the whole the more active, intelligent, and original men among the intellectuals who most frequently incline towards socialism, while its opponents are often of an inferior calibre. This is true particularly during the early stages of the infiltration of socialist ideas; later, although outside intellectual circles it may still be an act of courage to profess socialist convictions, the pressure of opinion among intellectuals will often be so strongly in favour of social-ism that it requires more strength and independence for a man to resist it than to join in what his fellows regard as modern views. Nobody, for instance, who is familiar with large numbers of university faculties (and from this point of view the majority of university teachers probably have to be classed as intellectuals rather than as experts) can remain oblivious to the fact that the most brilliant and successful teachers are today more likely than not to be socialists, while those who hold more conservative political views are as frequently mediocrities. This is of course by itself an important factor leading the younger generation into the socialist camp.

The socialist will, of course, see in this merely a proof that the more intelligent person is today bound to become a socialist. But this is far from being the necessary or even the most likely explanation. The main reason for this state of affairs is probably that, for the exceptionally able man who accepts the present order of society, a multitude of other avenues to influence and power are open, while to the disaffected and dissatisfied an intellectual career is the most promising path to both influence and the power to contribute to the achievement of his ideals. Even more than that: the more conservatively inclined man of first class ability will in general choose intellectual work (and the sacrifice in material reward which this choice usually entails) only if he enjoys it for its own sake. He is in consequence more likely to become an expert scholar rather than an intellectual in the specific sense of the word; while to the more radically minded the intellectual pursuit is more often than not a means rather than an end, a path to exactly that kind of wide influence which the professional intellectual exercises. It is therefore probably the fact, not that the more intelligent people are generally socialists, but that a much higher proportion of socialists among the best minds devote themselves to those intellectual pursuits which in modern society give them a decisive influence on public opinion.[3]

The selection of the personnel of the intellectuals is also closely connected with the predominant interest which they show in general and abstract ideas. Speculations about the possible entire reconstruction of society give the intellectual a fare much more to his taste than the more practical and short-run considerations of those who aim at a piecemeal improvement of the existing order. In particular, socialist thought owes its appeal to the young largely to its visionary character; the very courage to indulge in Utopian thought is in this respect a source of strength to the socialists which traditional liberalism sadly lacks. This difference operates in favour of socialism, not only because speculation about general principles provides an opportunity for the play of the imagination of those who are unencumbered by much knowledge of the facts of present-day life, but also because it satisfies a legitimate desire for the understanding of the rational basis of any social order and gives scope for the exercise of that constructive urge for which liberalism, after it had won its great victories, left few outlets. The intellectual, by his whole disposition, is uninterested in technical details or practical difficulties. What appeal to him are the broad visions, the specious comprehension of the social order as a whole which a planned system promises.

This fact that the tastes of the intellectual were better satisfied by the speculations of the socialists proved fatal to the influence of the liberal tradition. Once the basic demands of the liberal programmes seemed satisfied, the liberal thinkers turned to problems of detail and tended to neglect the development of the general philosophy of liberalism, which in consequence ceased to be a live issue offering scope for general speculation. Thus for something over half a century it has been only the socialists who have offered anything like an explicit programme of social development, a picture of the future society at which they were aiming, and a set of general principles to guide decisions on particular issues. Even though, if I am right, their ideals suffer from inherent contradictions, and any attempt to put them into practice must produce something utterly different from what they expect, this does not alter the fact that their programme for change is the only one which has actually influenced the development of social institutions. It is because theirs has become the only explicit general philosophy of social policy held by a large group, the only system or theory which raises new problems and opens new horizons, that they have succeeded in inspiring the imagination of the intellectuals.

The actual developments of society during this period were determined not by a battle of conflicting ideals, but by the contrast between an existing state of affairs and that one ideal of a possible future society which the socialists alone held up before the public. Very few of the other programmes which offered themselves provided genuine alternatives. Most of them were mere compromises or half-way houses between the more extreme types of socialism and the existing order. All that was needed to make almost any socialist proposal appear reasonable to these 'judicious' minds who were constitutionally convinced that the truth must always lie in the middle between the extremes, was for someone to advocate a sufficiently more extreme proposal. There seemed to exist only one direction in which we could move, and the only question seemed to be how fast and how far the movement should proceed.

VI

The significance of the special appeal to the intellectuals which socialism derives from its speculative character will become clearer if we further contrast the position of the socialist theorist with that of his counterpart who is a liberal in the old sense of the word. This comparison will also lead us to whatever lesson we can draw from an adequate appreciation of the intellectual forces which are undermining the foundations of a free society.

Paradoxically enough, one of the main handicaps which deprives the liberal thinker of popular influence is closely connected with the fact that, until socialism has actually arrived, he has more opportunity of directly influencing decisions on current policy and that in consequence he is not only not tempted into that long-run speculation which is the strength of the socialists, but is actually discouraged from it because any effort of this kind is likely to reduce the immediate good he can do. Whatever power he has to influence practical decisions he owes to his standing with the representatives of the existing order, and this standing he would endanger if he devoted himself to the kind of speculation which would appeal to the intellectuals and which through them could influence developments over longer periods. In order to carry weight with the powers that be, he has to be 'practical', 'sensible', and 'realistic'. So long as he concerns himself with immediate issues, he is rewarded with influence, material success, and popularity with those who up to a point share his general outlook. But these men have little respect for those speculations on general principles which shape the intellectual climate. Indeed, if he seriously indulges in such long-run speculation, he is apt to acquire the reputation of being 'unsound' or even half a socialist, because he is unwilling to identify the existing order with the free system at which he aims.[4]

If, in spite of this, his efforts continue in the direction of general speculation, he soon discovers that it is unsafe to associate too closely with those who seem to share most of his convictions, and he is soon driven into isolation. Indeed there can be few more thankless tasks at present than the essential one of developing the philosophical foundation on which the further development of a free society must be based. Since the man who undertakes it must accept much of the framework of the existing order, he will appear to many of the more speculatively minded intellectuals merely as a timid apologist of things as they are; at the same time he will be dismissed by the men of affairs as an impractical theorist. He is not radical enough for those who know only the world where 'with ease together dwell the thoughts' and much too radical for those who see only how 'hard in space together clash the things'. If he takes advantage of such support as he can get from the men of affairs, he will almost certainly discredit himself with those on whom he depends for the spreading of his ideas. At the same time he will need most carefully to avoid anything resembling extravagance or over-statement. While no socialist theorist has ever been known to discredit himself with his fellows even by the silliest of proposals, the old-fashioned liberal will damn himself by an impracticable suggestion. Yet for the intellectuals he will still not be speculative or adventurous enough, and the changes and improvements in the social structure he will have to offer will seem limited in comparison with what their less restrained imagination conceives.

At least in a society in which the main requisites of freedom have already been won and further improvements must concern points of comparative detail, the liberal programme can have none of the glamour of a new invention. The appreciation of the improvements it has to offer requires more knowledge of the working of the existing society than the average intellectual possesses. The discussion of these improvements must proceed on a more practical level than that of the more revolutionary programmes, thus giving a complexion which has little appeal for the intellectual and tending to bring in elements to whom he feels directly antagonistic. Those who are most familiar with the working of the present society are also usually interested in the preservation of particular features of that society which may not be defensible on general principles. Unlike the person who looks for an entirely new future order and who naturally turns for guidance to the theorist, the men who believe in the existing order also usually think that they understand it much better than any theorist and in consequence are likely to reject whatever is unfamiliar and theoretical.

The difficulty of finding genuine and disinterested support for a systematic policy for freedom is not new. In a passage of which the reception of a recent book of mine has often reminded me, Lord Acton long ago described how:

> at all times sincere friends of freedom have been rare, and its triumphs have been due to minorities, that have prevailed by associating themselves with auxiliaries whose objects differed from their own; and this association, which is always dangerous, has been sometimes disastrous, by giving to opponents just grounds of opposition...[5]

More recently, one of the most distinguished living American economists has complained in a similar vein that the main task of those who believe in the basic principles of the capitalist system must frequently be to defend this system against the capitalists—indeed the great liberal economists, from Adam Smith to the present, have always known this.

The most serious obstacle which separates the practical men who have the cause of freedom genuinely at heart from those forces which in the realm of ideas decide the course of development is their deep distrust of theoretical speculation and their tendency to orthodoxy; this, more than anything else, creates an almost impassable barrier between them and those intellectuals who are devoted to the same cause and whose assistance is indispensable if the cause is to prevail. Although this tendency is perhaps natural among men who defend a system because it has justified itself in practice, and to whom its intellectual justification seems immaterial, it is fatal to its survival because it deprives it of the support it most needs. Orthodoxy of any kind, any pretence that a system of ideas is final and must be unquestioningly accepted as a whole, is the one view which of necessity antagonises all intellectuals, whatever their views on particular issues. Any system which judges men by the completeness of their conformity to a fixed set of opinions, by their 'soundness' or the extent to which they can be relied upon to hold approved views on all points, deprives itself of a support without which no set of ideas can maintain its influence in modern society. The ability to criticise accepted views, to explore new vistas and to experiment with new conceptions, provides the atmosphere without which the intellectual cannot breathe. A cause which offers no scope for these traits can have no support from him and is thereby doomed in any society which, like ours, rests on his services.

VII

It may be that a free society as we have known it carries in itself the forces of its own destruction, that once freedom has been achieved it is taken for granted and ceases to be valued, and that the free growth of ideas which is the essence of a free society will bring about the destruction of the foundations on which it depends. There can be little doubt that in countries like the United States the ideal of freedom has today less real appeal for the young than it has in countries where they have learned what its loss means. On the other hand, there is every sign that in Germany and elsewhere, to the young men who have never known a free society, the task of constructing one can become as exciting and fascinating as any socialist scheme which has appeared during the last hundred years. It is an extraordinary fact, though one which many visitors have experienced, that in speaking to German students about the principles of a liberal society one finds a more responsive and even enthusiastic audience than one can hope to find in any of the Western democracies. In Britain also there is already appearing among the young a new interest in the principles of true liberalism which certainly did not exist a few years ago.

Does this mean that freedom is valued only when it is lost, that the world must everywhere go through a dark phase of socialist totalitarianism before the forces of freedom can gather strength anew? It may be so, but I hope it need not be. Yet, so long as the people who over longer periods determine public opinion continue to be attracted by the ideals of socialism, the trend will continue. If we are to avoid such a development, we must be able to offer a new liberal programme which appeals to the imagination. We must make the building of a free society once more an intellectual adventure, a deed of courage. What we lack is a liberal Utopia, a programme which seems neither a mere defence of things as they are nor a diluted kind of socialism, but a truly liberal radicalism which does not spare the susceptibilities of the mighty (including the trade unions), which is not too severely practical, and which does not confine itself to what appears today as politically possible. We need intellectual leaders who are prepared to resist the blandishments of power and influence and who are willing to work for an ideal, however small may be the prospects of its early realisation. They must be men who are willing to stick to principles and to fight for their full realisation, however remote. The practical compromises they must leave to the politicians. Free trade and freedom of opportunity are ideals which still may arouse the imaginations of large numbers, but a mere 'reasonable freedom of trade' or a mere 'relaxation of controls' is neither intellectually respectable nor likely to inspire any enthusiasm.

The main lesson which the true liberal must learn from the success of the socialists is that it was their courage to be Utopian which gained them the support of the intellectuals and therefore an influence on public opinion which is daily making possible what only recently seemed utterly remote. Those who have concerned themselves exclusively with what seemed practicable in the existing state of opinion have constantly found that even this has rapidly become politically impossible as the result of changes in a public opinion which they have done nothing to guide. Unless we can make the philosophic foundations of a free society once more a living intellectual issue, and its implementation a task which challenges the ingenuity and imagination of our liveliest minds, the prospects of freedom are indeed dark. But if we can regain that belief in the power of ideas which was the mark of liberalism at its best, the battle is not lost. The intellectual revival of liberalism is already under way in many parts of the world. Will it be in time?

Notes

John Blundell

1 Fisher, A., *Must History Repeat Itself?*, Churchill Press, 1974, p.103, quoted in Cockett, R., *Thinking the Unthinkable*, London: HarperCollins, 1995, pp.123-24.

2 Letter from Anthony Fisher to Oliver Smedley, 22 May 1956, quoted in Cockett, R., *op. cit.*, p. 131. Emphasis in original.

3 As Leonard P. Liggio, Executive Vice President of the Atlas Economic Research Foundation, often says, more people learn their economics from history than from economics.

4 Bennett, A., *Forty Years On*, first performance 31 October 1968, published London: Faber and Faber, 1969, p. 58.

5 Hayek, F., *The Fatal Conceit: The Errors of Socialism*, in Bartley, W.W. (ed.), *The Collected Works of Friedrich August Hayek*, London: Routledge, Vol. 1, 1988, pp. 52-54.

6 Review of *Contemporary Socialism* by John Rae, *Charity Organisation Review*, London: Charity Organisation Society, October 1885.

7 *New Labour: Because Britain Deserves Better*, London: The Labour Party, 1997. On the contrary, the manifesto complained that: 'Our system of government is centralised, inefficient and bureaucratic'.

8 Keynes, J.M., *The General Theory of Employment, Interest and Money*, London: Macmillan, p. 383.

9 Brash, D.T., *New Zealand's Remarkable Reforms*, Occasional Paper 100, London: Institute of Economic Affairs, 1996, p. 17.

F.A. Hayek

1 It would be interesting to discover how far a seriously critical view of the benefits to society of the law of copyright, or the expression of doubts about the public interest in the existence of a class which makes its living from the writing of books, would have a chance of being publicly stated in a society in which the channels of expression are so largely controlled by people who have a vested interest in the existing situation.

2 It was therefore not (as has been suggested by one reviewer of *The Road to Serfdom*, Professor J. Schumpeter) 'politeness to a fault' but profound conviction of the importance of this which made me, in Professor Schumpeter's words, 'hardly ever attribute to opponents anything beyond intellectual error'.

3   Related to this is another familiar phenomenon: there is little reason to believe that really first-class intellectual ability for original work is any rarer among Gentiles than among Jews. Yet there can be little doubt that men of Jewish stock almost everywhere constitute a disproportionately large number of the intellectuals in our sense, that is of the ranks of the professional interpreters of ideas. This may be their special gift and certainly is their main opportunity in countries where prejudice puts obstacles in their way in other fields. It is probably more because they constitute so large a proportion of the intellectuals than for any other reason that they seem to be so much more receptive to socialist ideas than people of different stocks.

4   The most glaring recent example of such condemnation of a somewhat unorthodox liberal work as 'socialist' has been provided by some comments on the late Henry Simons' *Economic Policy for a Free Society* (1948). One need not agree with the whole of this work and one may even regard some of the suggestions made in it as incompatible with a free society, and yet recognise it as one of the most important contributions made in recent times to our problem and as just the kind of work which is required to get discussion started on the fundamental issues. Even those who violently disagree with some of its suggestions should welcome it as a contribution which clearly and courageously raises the central problems of our time.

5   Acton, *The History of Freedom*, London, 1922.

Rediscovered Riches

An occasional series which seeks to inform and deepen the current debate on welfare reform by reprinting classic texts

The titles published so far:

Self-Help
by Samuel Smiles

Alexis de Tocqueville's
Memoir on Pauperism

Octavia Hill
and the Social Housing Debate
Essays and Letters by Octavia Hill

Self-Help
with illustrations of conduct and perseverance

by Samuel Smiles

Rediscovered Riches Series No. 1
ISBN 0-255 36365-6
Price £9.00. Published June 1996

First published in 1859, *Self-Help* used the inspiring stories of hundreds of individuals who had overcome great obstacles to convey its central message—that success owes little to birth or fortune, but depends almost entirely on hard work and perseverance in the face of setbacks. Smiles believed that we should not look to the state to solve our problems for us, when most of them could be addressed by the exercise of ordinary virtues like industry, thrift and self-restraint, which are within the grasp of everyone. In the context of the current debate about the de-moralising effects of the welfare state, *Self-Help* seems as relevant today as the day it was published.

'The message of this book, which is readable and full of stunning quotations, is: God helps those who help themselves. A century after Smiles' death we have had to learn this all over again—the hard way.'

Paul Johnson, *The Daily Mail*

'Sound sentiments, finely expressed...The IEA sees [*Self-Help*] as a blueprint for a social and political consensus based on a radical downsizing of the state.'

The Guardian

'As a storyteller [Smiles] is vivid, most of all when he conjures up the industrial revolutionaries: Wedgwood, Watt, Arkwright, George Stephenson and even Jonas Hanway, who taught City men the habit of carrying umbrellas.'

Christopher Fildes, *The Spectator*

'Samuel Smiles is alive and well and available to lead us into the next decade...The Victorian moralist's universal best-seller...is a better guide to the prevailing political and economic orthodoxy than the incomprehensible texts of that other 19th century thinker, Karl Marx.'

Joe Rogaly, *The Financial Times*

Alexis de Tocqueville's Memoir on Pauperism

translated by Seymour Drescher
with an introduction by Gertrude Himmelfarb

Rediscovered Riches Series No. 2

ISBN 0-255 36394-X

Price £5.00. Published May 1997

Visiting England in 1833, Alexis de Tocqueville, most famous for his great classic *Democracy in America*, was shocked by the number of people dependent on the poor law—estimated by him as one in six of the population. He argued that Britain, then the richest country in Europe, had more paupers than other countries just because it was so rich. Things regarded as luxuries in poor countries were necessities to the British, and they were not prepared to see their fellow countrymen sink into want amidst plenty. Thus the British Poor Law, established by Elizabeth I, made Britain the first country in the world to have a universal, rights-based welfare system which guaranteed an income to all who claimed it.

In her introduction, Gertrude Himmelfarb, one of the foremost historians of the nineteenth century, shows the relevance of Tocqueville's insights for the modern debate about welfare reform in both Britain and America.

Alexis de Tocqueville delivered his 'Memoir on Pauperism' as a speech in 1835. This English translation is now published for the first time in Britain.

'Britain's culture of dependency stretched back to the Elizabethan poor laws, [Tocqueville] claimed...Can Field and Harman reverse not just 50 years of dependency, but centuries of it?'

The Sunday Times

Octavia Hill
and the Social Housing Debate
Essays and Letters by Octavia Hill

Edited and with an introduction by
Robert Whelan

Rediscovered Riches Series No. 3

ISBN 0-255 36431-8

Price £7.00. Published February 1998

Octavia Hill (1838-1912) was famous for her work among the poor, particularly in the field of housing. She would take over properties, often in the worst areas, complete with their existing tenants, and set about improving tenants and tenements together. She insisted that her tenants, poor as they were, must pay their way. By the time of her death she was managing nearly two thousand houses and flats, including large estates belonging to the Ecclesiastical Commissioners. Her work for the poor included the open spaces movement and she was one of the co-founders of the National Trust.

Octavia Hill wrote little for publication, and has been out of print for most of this century. This selection of her writings and talks (some never published before) seeks to deepen debate by drawing on the lessons of the last century.

'This extremely useful book...is well worth reading...Many of Octavia Hill's ideas have important implications, particularly in terms of the current debate about anti-social behaviour, and would repay being widely discussed and thought about.'

Housing

'Octavia Hill wrote with the confidence of the autonomous voluntary worker who knew what she was talking about...The relevance of her example to the dilemma we now face is immediately apparent.'

Community Care

'Ironically, in view of the criticisms which have been levied at her, she seems more relevant than ever in the modern welfare debate.'

Housing Agenda